SOMALIA SEATON

Somalia Seaton is a British-Jamaican and Nigerian playwright and screenwriter, born and raised in South-East London.

She is a 2017 Susan Smith Blackburn Prize finalist, with her play *Fall of the Kingdom, Rise of the Footsoldier*. Her debut play *Crowning Glory* was shortlisted for the 2014 Alfred Fagon Award.

Writing credits include *Fall of the Kingdom, Rise of the Footsoldier* (RSC); *House* (Clean Break; Assembly Rooms, Edinburgh/The Yard, London); *Crowning Glory* (Stratford East); *Curly Fries and Bass* (Lyric, Hammersmith); *Mama's Little Angel* (The Yard, London); *Hush Little Baby* (Open Works Theatre Co./Soho Theatre).

Other Plays for Young People to Perform from Nick Hern Books

Original Plays

100
Christopher Heimann,
   Neil Monaghan, Diene Petterle

BANANA BOYS
Evan Placey

BLOOD AND ICE
Liz Lochhead

BOYS
Ella Hickson

BRAINSTORM
Ned Glasier, Emily Lim
   and Company Three

BUNNY
Jack Thorne

BURYING YOUR BROTHER
   IN THE PAVEMENT
Jack Thorne

COCKROACH
Sam Holcroft

DISCO PIGS
Enda Walsh

EIGHT
Ella Hickson

THE FALL
James Fritz

GIRLS LIKE THAT
Evan Placey

HOLLOWAY JONES
Evan Placey

I CAUGHT CRABS IN WALBERSWICK
Joel Horwood

MOGADISHU
Vivienne Franzmann

MOTH
Declan Greene

THE MYSTAE
Nick Whitby

OVERSPILL
Ali Taylor

PRONOUN
Evan Placey

SAME
Deborah Bruce

THE URBAN GIRL'S GUIDE TO
   CAMPING AND OTHER PLAYS
Fin Kennedy

THE WARDROBE
Sam Holcroft

Adaptations

ANIMAL FARM
Ian Wooldridge
Adapted from George Orwell

ARABIAN NIGHTS
Dominic Cooke

BEAUTY AND THE BEAST
Laurence Boswell

CORAM BOY
Helen Edmundson
Adapted from Jamila Gavin

DAVID COPPERFIELD
Alastair Cording
Adapted from Charles Dickens

GREAT EXPECTATIONS
Nick Ormerod and Declan Donnellan
Adapted from Charles Dickens

HIS DARK MATERIALS
Nicholas Wright
Adapted from Philip Pullman

THE JUNGLE BOOK
Stuart Paterson
Adapted from Rudyard Kipling

KENSUKE'S KINGDOM
Stuart Paterson
Adapted from Michael Morpurgo

KES
Lawrence Till
Adapted from Barry Hines

NOUGHTS & CROSSES
Dominic Cooke
Adapted from Malorie Blackman

THE RAILWAY CHILDREN
Mike Kenny
Adapted from E. Nesbit

SWALLOWS AND AMAZONS
Helen Edmundson and Neil Hannon
Adapted from Arthur Ransome

TO SIR, WITH LOVE
Ayub Khan-Din
Adapted from E.R Braithwaite

TREASURE ISLAND
Stuart Paterson
Adapted from Robert Louis Stevenson

WENDY & PETER PAN
Ella Hickson
Adapted from J.M. Barrie

THE WOLVES OF WILLOUGHBY
   CHASE
Russ Tunney
Adapted from Joan Aiken

Somalia Seaton

RED

NICK HERN BOOKS
www.nickhernbooks.co.uk

TONIC THEATRE
www.tonictheatre.co.uk

A Nick Hern Book

Red first published as a paperback original in Great Britain in 2017 by Nick Hern Books Limited, The Glasshouse, 49a Goldhawk Road, London W12 8QP, in association with Tonic

Red copyright © 2017 Somalia Seaton

Somalia Seaton has asserted her right to be identified as the author of this work

Cover image by Kathy Barber, Bullet Creative, www.bulletcreative.com

Designed and typeset by Nick Hern Books, London
Printed and bound in Great Britain by Mimeo Ltd, Huntingdon, Cambridgeshire PE29 6XX

A CIP catalogue record for this book is available from the British Library

ISBN   978 1 84842 652 8

Woodland CARBON
www.woodlandcarbon.co.uk
NICK HERN BOOKS
Printed on Carbon Captured paper

Contents

THE GLOVE THIEF
BY BETH FLINTOFF

PLATFORM

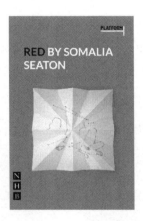

RED BY SOMALIA
SEATON

PLATFORM

THE LIGHT BURNS
BLUE BY SILVA
SEMERCIYAN

PLATFORM

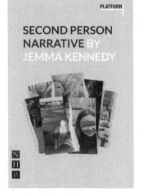

SECOND PERSON
NARRATIVE BY
JEMMA KENNEDY

PLATFORM

THIS CHANGES
EVERYTHING BY
JOEL HORWOOD

PLATFORM

PLATFORM

Commissioning and publishing a range of new plays which give girls a greater share of the action was always on my to-do list when I founded Tonic in 2011. While Tonic has very big aspirations – to support theatre in the UK to achieve greater gender equality – it is a small company and so we have to make careful choices about where we target our efforts. I spend lots of time looking to identify 'pressure points' – places where, with a bit of work, a great effect can be achieved. For this reason, much of Tonic's work focuses on partnerships with some of the largest theatres in the country, because if they change, others will follow. But it has always been clear to me that youth drama is one of the greatest pressure points of all. It is the engine room of the theatre industry; tomorrow's theatre-makers (not to mention audience members) are to be found today in youth-theatre groups, university drama societies and school drama clubs all over the country. If we can challenge their assumptions about the role of women's stories, voices, and ideas in drama, then change in the profession – in time – will be immeasurably easier to achieve.

Beyond this strategic interest in youth drama, I was convinced that girls were getting a raw deal, and I found that troubling. Having worked previously as a youth-theatre director, I was familiar with the regular challenge of trying to find scripts that had adequate numbers of female roles for all the committed and talented girls that wanted to take part. In nearly all the various youth-drama groups I worked in across a five-year period, there were significantly more girls than boys. However, when it came to finding big-cast, age-appropriate plays for them to work on, I was constantly frustrated by how few there seemed to be that provided enough opportunity for the girls. When looking at contemporary new writing for young actors to perform, one could be mistaken for thinking that youth drama was a predominantly male pursuit, rather than the other way round.

Aside from the practicalities of matching the number of roles to
the number of girls in any one drama group, the nature of writing
for female characters was something I struggled to get excited
about. While there were some notable examples, often the
writing for female characters seemed somewhat lacklustre. They
tended to be characters at the periphery of the action rather than
its heart, with far less to say and do than their male counterparts,
and with a tendency towards being one-dimensional, rather than
complex or vibrant, funny or surprising. Why was it that in the
twenty-first century, the *quality* as well as the *quantity* of roles
being written for girls still seemed to lag behind those for boys?

Keen to check I wasn't just imagining this imbalance, Tonic
conducted a nationwide research study looking into
opportunities for girls in youth drama, focusing on the quantity
and quality of roles available to them. The research was written
up into a report, *Swimming in the shallow end*, and
is published on the Tonic website. Not only did the research
confirm my worst fears, more depressingly, it exceeded them.
Many of the research participants were vocal about the social,
artistic and emotional benefits that participation in youth-drama
productions can have on a young person's life. But so too were
they – to quote the report – on 'the erosion to self-esteem,
confidence and aspiration when these opportunities are
repeatedly held out of reach... [and] for too many girls, this is
the case'.

But despite the doom and gloom of the research findings, there
remained an exciting proposition; to write stories that weren't
currently being put on stage, and to foreground – rather than
ignore – the experiences, achievements and world-view of
young women, perhaps the group above all others in our society
whose situation has altered so dramatically over the past
hundred or so years. The brief Tonic sets Platform writers is:
write a large-cast play specifically for performance by young
actors, with mainly or entirely female casts and in which the
female characters are no less complex or challenging than the
male characters. We ask them to write in such a way that these
plays can be performed by young people anywhere in the
country, and that there should be scope for every school, college

and youth-theatre group performing the play to make a production their own.

There are now five Platform plays published, of which this is one, and our hope is that there will be many more. Our aspiration – fundraising permitting – is to keep commissioning titles in the series so that over time, Platform will become a new canon of writing for young actors, and one that puts girls and their lives centre stage. The first three plays in the series were published two years ago and already in that time have been performed across the length and breadth of the United Kingdom, as well as in Ireland, Australia and the USA. I look forward to hearing about productions of this play, and a future where great stories about girls and their lives are being staged in theatres, halls, drama studios and classrooms as the rule rather than the exception.

Lucy Kerbel
Director, Tonic

www.tonictheatre-platform.co.uk

Acknowledgements

Tonic would like to thank:

Matt Applewhite, Tamara von Werthern, Jon Barton, Marcelo Dos Santos and all at Nick Hern Books, Moira Buffini, Company Three, Rose Bruford College of Theatre & Performance, the National Youth Theatre of Great Britain, and the National Theatre Studio.

We are grateful to the following for their support of Platform:

The Chapman Charitable Trust, Didymus, Garrick Charitable Trust, Golsoncott Foundation, John Thaw Foundation, and Unity Theatre Trust.

THE GOLSONCOTT FOUNDATION

Tonic was created in 2011 to support the theatre industry to achieve greater gender equality in its workforces and repertoires. Today, Tonic partners with leading theatres and performing-arts organisations around the UK on a range of projects, schemes and creative works. Current and recent partners include Chichester Festival Theatre, English Touring Theatre, National Theatre, New Wolsey Theatre, Northern Ballet, Royal Opera House, Royal Shakespeare Company, Sadler's Wells, West Yorkshire Playhouse, and the Young Vic.

Tonic's approach involves getting to grips with the principles that lie beneath how our industry functions – our working methods, decision-making processes, and organisational structures – and identifying how, in their current form, these can create barriers. Once we have done that, we devise practical yet imaginative alternative approaches and work with our partners to trial and deliver them. Essentially, our goal is to equip our colleagues in UK theatre with the tools they need to ensure more talented women are given the opportunity to rise to the top.

Platform is a collaboration between Tonic and Nick Hern Books. Nick Hern Books also publishes Tonic's books: *100 Great Plays for Women* and *All Change Please: A Practical Guide to Achieving Gender Equality in Theatre*.

www.tonictheatre.co.uk

N H B Nick Hern Books

Theatre publishers & performing rights agents

We leapt at the chance to publish and license the Platform plays in collaboration with Tonic, and always had high hopes that by making plays available which gave young women the opportunity to take centre stage, we would improve not only their confidence levels, but also start to have a positive effect on the theatrical landscape as a whole.

After all, here at the Performing Rights Department at Nick Hern Books, we're often asked, 'Are there any plays for young people?'... 'Have you got anything for a large cast?'... and 'Is there anything with strong female roles?'

Whilst the answer to these questions is, in each case, a resounding 'Yes!' (and in fact the majority of plays we've published in recent years have been by women), the number of plays that fulfil all three of these criteria – strong roles for a large, predominantly or all-female cast of young actors – has historically been less plentiful. Yet that's where there's so much demand! Nearly every teacher and youth-theatre director in the country knows that it's girls who make up the majority of their casts, and yet the plays available are often dominated by men. Because we can generally only publish what is being produced on the professional stages of the UK, until the theatre industry starts staging more plays with these qualities, the numbers will remain low. It's a vicious circle.

Two years after the publication of the first three Platform plays in 2015, I am delighted to report that this circle has somewhat started to disintegrate. It's a source of great pleasure that, aside from their social and political purpose, they're all excellent plays in their own right. As such, we have licensed dozens of productions of the Platform plays to date, providing opportunities and great roles to hundreds of young women (and young men, for that matter) around the world. While this is cause for celebration, it is no reason for complacency – the journey continues – and we are delighted to publish two great new Platform plays, which will hopefully be received as enthusiastically by schools and youth-theatre groups as the first three in the series.

Nick Hern Books looks after the amateur performing rights to over a thousand plays, and we know from experience that when it comes to choosing the right play it can be confusing (and pricey) to read enough of what's out there until you know which play is right for you. This is why we send out approval copies: up to three plays at a time, for thirty days, after which they have to be paid for, or returned to us in mint condition, and you just need to pay the postage. So there is no reason not to read all of the available Platform plays to see if they will suit your school, college or youth-theatre group. We're very hopeful that one of them will.

Performing rights to all five Platform plays are available at a specially reduced rate to enable even those on a very tight budget to perform them. Discounts are also available on cast sets of scripts; and the cover images on these books can be supplied, free of charge, for you to use on your poster.

If you have any questions about Platform, or any of the plays on our list, or want to talk about what you're looking for, we are always happy to speak with you. Call us on +44 (0)20 8749 4953, or email us at rights@nickhernbooks.co.uk.

And here's to many more Platform plays in the future!

Tamara von Werthern
Performing Rights Manager
Nick Hern Books

www.nickhernbooks.co.uk/plays-to-perform

Introduction
Somalia Seaton

With *Red*, I wanted to interrogate the reasons behind the catastrophic number of young people that are reported missing in the UK. Seventy young people are reported missing in London alone, every single day. I had thought that I would write a play about this, then I thought I was writing a play about how young people empower themselves by metaphorically disappearing themselves in spaces not right for them...

But what I was really writing was a play about grief. A play that looks at the debris left behind when someone leaves. A play that looks at how a young girl learns to cope with no longer having her closest friend by her side. I wanted to look at the power of our minds and how we create mini-worlds in there, that wrap their arms around us and keep us comforted from the harsh realities of the outside. *Red* is about friendship, loss, girlhood and grief.

Acknowledgements

There have been many practitioners involved in the development of *Red*, notably Jane Fallowfield and the following theatre-makers from Company Three: Aaliyah Murrian, Abigail Phillips-Douglas, Alannah Makoni, Anisha Ngagba, Arianna King, Bailey Smith, Cherie Duah, Cynthia Mumbaya, Danielle Maragh, Dylan Lubo, Fransisco Rodrigues, Inaayat Chowdhury, Isobel Burrows, Jack Hughes, Jaekwan Hunte-Jarrett, Jake Monib, James-Leon Gallacher, Jonathan Gini Rodrigues, Kadiesat Turay, Kayne Parara, Nusayba Abaas, Olga Popiolek-Szulczewska, Selin Goksungar, Sonya Miah and Vini Padoan. With further contributions from the following: Allyson Brown, Rebecca Omogbehin, Sophia Jackson, Sheri-An Davis, Sasha Frost, Urielle Klein-Mekongo, Rosie Wyatt, Jacoba Williams, Camilla Stanger, Suzie Kirk Dumitru, Jen Thomas, Anna Niland and the National Youth Theatre.

Many thanks to Lucy Kerbel, Ned Glasier, Adam Coleman, Maa-Yarkor Addo and Segen Yosef.

S.S.

Production Note

The Text

Where / appears there is an overlap in speech.

Where lines and words appear within [ ] they are not to be spoken.

Set

The set should feel sparse and mystical.

Familiar objects may appear on stage, but in some obscure way. It is very possible to disregard the use of noted props.

The World

Dusk: The moment between Day and Night, when the sky looks various shades of reds. These scenes are Dee's version of events, but her recalling of memories may not always be factually accurate.

Day/Night: It is suggested that these are two alternative states to Dusk. Scenes that take place during Day are in real time.

The Chorus

The Chorus are everywhere at all times, and should feel present throughout the play.

Sometimes, and more often than not, they are our gateway into Dee's grief. They know more than us and more than the other characters in the play. Sometimes they embody those other characters, i.e. Jay and Mother.

The Chorus can speak in unison, or individually. It is important for each company to develop a personality or several for the Chorus.

Adults are felt but never seen, especially during Dusk scenes.

RED

Characters

DEE
JAY
BEE
TEE
GEE

CHORUS

MOTHER, *voice-over*

One

Dusk.

The Tent.

DEE *is visibly anxious. She checks her phone and keeps an eye out. A sack appears out of nowhere. She opens up the sack to reveal a tent. She begins setting it up. It does not need to be big, it could be symbolic, it could be miniature. It needs to be practical and easy to assemble. Once it's assembled, she takes off her trainers, and undoes her school tie. She lays down on the grass and runs her hands and feet through it and looks up at the sky.*

DEE *flashes her torch inside her tent, making shapes and keeping a lookout. Outside we hear* MOTHER, *though we never see her.*

MOTHER. She won't come out.

Doesn't matter how hard you try, she won't come out.

I've asked her friends, I've spoken to the school, they all say the same thing.

She's in shock.

Give her time.

Let her be.

But, I'm worried, I'm worried I'm gonna lose my little girl, I'm worried she'll never speak again, like I've lost my grip, like she's...

We become aware of the CHORUS *darting throughout the space.*

...floating far far away from me, and I'll never hold her again, or be able to tell her it's okay, I'm here.

CHORUS. Like she'll never trust that I can protect her from the pain she's feeling now. I just wanna wrap her in my arms and take it all away. But they say –

She's in shock.

Give her time.

Let her be.

Will you… will you just go and speak to her…

Please?

Could you just try and get her to say something?

Please?

I need her to come out from there, just for a little while.

Just so I know she's with us, ya know?

Here with us.

You understand?

Right?

Two

Dusk.

We are inside DEE*'s mind. It is always Dusk in her mind and the sky is always red. (It might be that you represent this with light or it might be that you represent this with cloth. It might be that you choose not to represent this at all. Any of these choices are fine.)*

JAY *appears.*

JAY (*whispers*). Psst! Psst!

Come on!

DEE. Jay?

JAY. Yes! Hurry up!

DEE. What are you doing?

JAY. Breaking you out! You've turned into a right bore!

DEE. I don't understand where you've been.

JAY. I can't tell you.

DEE. Why?

JAY. Because 'Y' has two arms and a leg!

DEE. What?!

JAY. You look like crap!

DEE. I don't!

JAY. There's no life behind your eyes.

DEE. It's been difficult.

JAY. Get over yourself!

DEE. I shouldn't even be talking to you.

JAY. Fine! Bye!

DEE. Where are you going?

JAY. I've got a race in like thirty seconds.

DEE. What?

JAY. Hurry up!

JAY bolts outside and takes her position at the starting line.

DEE. Wait!

DEE reluctantly peeps out of the tent and notices the CROWD.

In this scene we watch JAY *racing. The* CHORUS *become the* CROWD. *Some cheer her on, some don't. The* CHORUS *find individual characters in how they stand, how they cheer.*

CHORUS. On your mark.

> JAY *takes her position.*

Get set!

GO!!

The CROWD *cheers.*

JAY races back and forth, she is winning the race and she knows it.

The CROWD *love her.*

And she loves the CROWD.

Did you know there are like seven billion people on Earth?

Well, seven-point-five.

There are seven-point-five billion people on planet Earth.

As far as we know.

JAY starts to run out of breath.

That's... nuts!

I mean.

What does that even look like?

Like how can your brain even see that?

JAY starts to slow down.

The CROWD *cheer her on and* JAY *gains momentum again.*

Like how can your brain even comprehend that?

Or even, hold that information...

What would we even do with that information?

If we could really understand it?

Contain it... hold it or... comprehend it...

Would we... try to connect more?

Become realigned...

Because, it's huge.

The idea that there are seven-point-five, or there are seven billion four hundred ninety-nine million nine hundred ninety-nine thousand nine hundred ninety-nine others... walking around, holding what I'm holding, trying not to fall down... and with all this, can you ever really know someone?

Know what makes them feel immense joy and excruciating pain?

Can you actually ever really successfully help someone?

Be there for someone, when you're holding all of this...

It's like...

You wanna say all these things like...

You plan to say all these things that hold meaning...

But your tongue gets caught on a...

What exactly?

Something... sharp!

Something like...

I guess...

What's the best way to say...

A hook!!

Yeah! It's like...

Suspended from the roof of ya mouth...

JAY's struggling again, she's running out of air, she's slowing down.

Sounds uncomfortable.

And that's what I mean... I think.

No one wants a hook in their mouth…

Blocking their need to speak / and…

And then imagine if your fingers didn't work and you couldn't remove it.

And the muscles in your mouth had gone all floppy so you had to make sounds…

In an attempt to communicate…

To convey all of this… [everything-ness].

Move your eyes up and down to convey all of this…

You'd do anything…

To be able to say…

To communicate…

To share… or at least try to share the message…

…your message.

Sent from your brain to your mouth…

JAY *comes to a halt, bends down to catch her breath.*

To all seven-point-five billion of us…

In an attempt to connect.

An attempt to understand, to help, to save.

She wants to save her friend.

She wants to.

To communicate all of this…

Everything-ness to her friend, to make her feel whole again.

JAY *finishes the race, falls to her knees and bursts into a fit of laughter, and the* CHORUS *do too.*

Three

Dusk.

We are in a cul-de sac. It is the stomping ground for the GIRLS *and the general setting for the play. There may be movement outside of the main action between the* GIRLS *during this scene.*

BEE, TEE, GEE, JAY and DEE, and the CHORUS *run through the cul-de-sac trying not to laugh – and failing. Trying to hide – and failing. Each of them find a really rubbish hiding spot and freeze.*

TEE. Your turn!

JAY. No way.

BEE. Yes way!

JAY. What about you?

DEE. Don't be a spoilsport, Rhino.

JAY. Please!!!

GEE. It's your turn or it's a forfeit.

JAY. No!

GEE. It's a forfeit, you can't say no!

JAY. I don't want to do that, it's stupid.

DEE. You're being such a brat.

JAY. I'm not, I'm uncomfortable.

DEE. It's not supposed to be comfortable, you idiot!

JAY. Ergh! Whatever! Which door?

BEE *points with excitement.*

BEE. That one!

TEE. No way!!!

DEE. Genius!

JAY. I'm not doing that!!!

GEE. Forfeit it is then!!

DEE. Come on! Up you get!

JAY. She's insane!

DEE. Don't be ridiculous!

JAY. I'm not doing it!

BEE. Fine, don't. Two laps round the car park without your school shirt on then!

They laugh.

JAY. You've got to be kidding me!

DEE. Let's not get distracted here!

(*To* JAY.) You're gonna knock on that door and then you're gonna hide behind that bush!

Right? Right?

JAY. Ergh! Fine!

The GIRLS *creep around the outskirts of the cul-de-sac trying not to be seen.*

JAY *arrives at the front door, looks back to her friends. Each of them gesture for her to knock.*

JAY *knocks.*

No answer.

JAY (*whispers back to the* GIRLS). There's no one in!

TEE. Knock again!

JAY *knocks.*

The GIRLS *duck back down.*

They wait.

JAY. Someone's coming!!

The door opens.

JAY *ducks.*

The door closes.

The GIRLS *all laugh.*

JAY *emerges again.*

She knocks again.

This time the door opens and the neighbour's feet are heard walking down the path.

JAY *sneaks into the house and slams the door behind her. The neighbour is now locked out and we hear them banging on the door.*

The GIRLS *emerge from their hiding spots, laughing, they goad the neighbour.*

The neighbour begins to chase after the GIRLS. *They run in different directions.*

TEE. Run!!!

The neighbour continues.

BEE *is struck by something.*

BEE. OW!!!

GEE. What was that?

DEE. Run for cover!!!

They dive behind a wall.

At a point, TEE's *head emerges.*

TEE. I can see Jay!

GEE. Run!!!

TEE. Oh my gosh!

DEE. Run, Jay, run!!!

BEE. Leave her alone!!!

DEE. Get off of her, you loser!!!

GEE. Run, Jay! Run!!

TEE. OVER HERE!!!

JAY *dives down next to her friends.*

DEE. Sssh!!!

GEE. Are you hurt?

JAY. No!

GEE. You looked like you were dancing!

DEE. She was ducking and diving!

JAY. I fly like a butterfly, sting like a bee! I gave her Ali!

The GIRLS *crack up.*

BEE. Did you get anything?

JAY. Maybe!!!

TEE. She didn't!

JAY. So what's this then?!

JAY *pulls out a small framed painting. They all gasp.*

TEE. What the hell!

GEE. You were in there for like a second!

JAY. It's Muhammad Ali to you.

DEE. Hands down, the best that ever did it!!!

BEE. How did you manage that?

JAY. First thing I saw on the wall!

DEE. What is it?

JAY. I dunno, a woman walking towards the sea.

GEE. Towards the sky more like.

JAY. See, that's the thing, the sky and the sea look the same.

TEE. She's walking towards something.

JAY. She's not walking, she's running.

DEE. Towards what, though?

GEE. She looks bonkers if you ask me.

TEE. She looks serene.

BEE. She looks lost.

JAY. Maybe she just got up one day and decided she wanted to leave.

TEE. That's a bit deep, but whatever.

JAY. I really like it.

DEE. Me too.

Four

Night.

CHORUS. So there's this game, and it's a bit weird.

Well, it's not weird, it's just… perhaps a bit dangerous.

Has the capacity to be dangerous…

If you were to, like… lose sense of where you are, or time or something.

Like… if you got confused by what was a game and what was actually real, then perhaps then, someone could be forgiven for referring to it as dangerous.

I don't really wanna say any more...

Well, it's just a bit...

Weird...

It's awkward not weird... she's not weird... she's struggling, I guess.

We're all struggling but, I guess.

This is how she copes.

How she needs to cope.

I've said too much...

Gotta go!

Five

Dusk.

The cul-de sac. We see the community surrounding this space: everyone knows each other, and nobody minds their own business. Sometimes the murmur of several televisions can be heard.

Perhaps everyone is arriving back home from work. Perhaps some greet each other. Perhaps there's a nosey or overfamiliar neighbour stopping a grumpy neighbour from getting in to watch the news. Perhaps we see who the families are and what corners of the stage their homes are set. Maybe the stage is empty apart from DEE *and* JAY. *Maybe the entire company is on stage watching them, or at least passing by as the scene goes on.*

JAY *pushes* DEE *around in a trolley. They are full of joy.*

The CHORUS *watch on.*

DEE. I want to go faster!!!

JAY. I'm trying!!

DEE. Try harder!!

JAY. I am!!!

DEE. Move your feet faster then!!

JAY. I am!

DEE. Even faster!

JAY. What if they fall off?!

DEE. They can't fall off.

JAY. But what if they do?

DEE. Then you have mankier feet than I thought!

JAY. My feet are beautiful!

DEE. They're dry like rhinoceros skin!

JAY. Shut ya face!

DEE. As dry as the Sahara!

JAY. You haven't even been to the Sahara!

DEE. Doesn't stop your feet being as dry as it!

JAY. Like your breath!

DEE. Like your foot!!

JAY. Like your lip in the winter!

DEE. LIKE YOUR RHINO FOOT! Spin me, Rhinoceros! Spin me round and round until my head rolls away from my neck!

JAY. You're so stupid!!!

    JAY *spins the trolley round.*

DEE. You're moving too slow!

JAY. Alright!

DEE. FASTER!!!

JAY. Shut up!

DEE. FASTER!

JAY. ALRIGHT!!!

DEE. And...

JAY. I can't go faster...

DEE....And stop!!!

JAY *stops*.

I HEREBY...

JAY. Ssssh! You're gonna get us caught!

DEE. No rations for you this week! Guards! Guards, take her away!!!

JAY. Seriously!!!

DEE. BOTHERED!!!

JAY. You're a clown!

DEE. I beg your pardon?

JAY. Dearest Merciful One...

DEE. Yes, dear?

JAY. May I possibly have the chance to spineth liketh no oneth haseth evereth doneth beforeth?

They burst into laughter.

DEE. What was that?

JAY. Shakespeare / obviously...

DEE. It's not bloody Shakes/peare...

JAY. It's SHAKESPEEEEARE...

DEE. You can't just talk in gibberish and...

JAY. SHAKESPEEEEEEARE!!!

DEE. You can't call it Shakespeare, it's barely even English.

JAY. I'm calling it Shakespeare.

DEE. It's not a language!

JAY. Shakespearean.

DEE. Shakespearean language?

JAY. Yes!

DEE. That's just stupid!

JAY. Shakespearean!

Like Egyptian! Like... Latin!

DEE. I can't even be bothered!

JAY. 'Cause I'm right.

DEE. 'Cause it's literally up there with the top-five dumbest things I have ever heard come out of your mouth!

JAY. I'm right, though!

DEE. You're not right!

JAY. My turn!!

DEE. No! You've barely pushed me.

JAY. What?

DEE. And I didn't finish my queen speech.

JAY. It was crap anyway!

DEE. Maybe I'll turn her into a character.

JAY. A character?

DEE. Yep! Next time Ms Darcy asks us who we've observed in our communities, maybe I'll say, 'A queen, Ms Darcy, I observed a queen, who walks amongst the peasants of the land, a graceful queen who takes pity on stupid friends who says stupid things!'

JAY. Could you imagine? 'Oh darling, such fine character work, such graciousness in your stage presence, oh darling!'

DEE. Move like a tree, darling!

JAY. Think of your Laban, darling!

DEE. More fluid, darling!!

JAY. What's her 'want', darling?

DEE. What does the Queen want, darling?

JAY. Does she fall in love with a peasant, darling?

DEE. Oh yes, darling!

JAY. She falls in love, darling!

DEE. Perhaps you should move like the wind!

Yes! Let's all move like the wind! Let's do it with her! Come on, schweeties! Let's all move like the wind! Roar like the wind! I am the wind! I am the roar in the wind! I am Earth Mother! Empress of the Clouds! Goddess of the Sea! I am Ms Darcy of the Darconians! One generation removed from God!

JAY. She wouldn't go that far!

DEE. Yeah, she would, she's a failed actress desperate for the limelight!

JAY. A bit harsh.

DEE. Not really.

JAY. I like her.

DEE. Me too, but come on!

JAY. She's alright!

DEE. She's weird!

JAY. She's not that weird!

DEE. If you say so.

JAY. She cares about people.

DEE. Please! She cares about herself.

JAY. That's not true.

DEE. Well… whatever!

JAY. She wrote me a letter one time.

DEE. For what?

JAY. …Just did.

DEE. Why?

JAY. Well… That time I was off school…

DEE. What like every other week?

JAY. No.

DEE. So what did this mystery letter say then?

JAY. Nothing.

DEE. What?

JAY. I dunno.

DEE. What do you mean, 'dunno'?

JAY. I can't remember.

DEE. You're lying.

JAY. Fine. Are you gonna let me in there or not?

DEE. Don't change / the subject.

JAY. It doesn't matter.

DEE. Well, then why did you mention it?

JAY. I just did.

DEE. So then why / stop?

JAY. Because I did, and that's that.

DEE. We tell each other everything.

JAY. Do we?

DEE. Yeah.

Beat.

JAY. Boring!

DEE. You're being really annoying.

JAY *jumps in the trolley with* DEE.

JAY. Spin me, peasant one!

DEE. Stop being a weirdo, come on!

JAY. SPIN ME!

DEE. We're in the middle of a conversation.

DEE *jumps out of the trolley.*

JAY. *You* were. Now you're spinning me!

DEE *starts spinning* JAY.

DEE. You're acting strange.

JAY. Am not.

DEE. What was I supposed to have known?

JAY. Faster!

DEE. I missed something, wasn't paying attention.

JAY. SPIIIIIN MEEEE!

DEE. Stop shouting in my ear!

JAY. You're moving too slow!!!

DEE. Faster than you did!!!

DEE *picks up the pace.*

JAY. FASTER!!!

JAY *loses her balance.*

FASTER!!!

FASTER!!!

FASTER!!!

DEE *lets go of the trolley and* JAY *spirals away, screaming with joy.*

DEE. BLAST OFF!!!

Both of them crash into a heap of laughter.

JAY. See you tomorrow, Rhinoceros.

DEE. See you tomorrow.

JAY. Don't forget the tent.

DEE. Jay.

JAY. What?

DEE. Did I miss something?

JAY. Goodnight, babe.

DEE. Goodnight, Rhinoceros.

JAY. Look at the sky!! It's mental!!!

Six

Dusk.

The Tent.

DEE *takes off her trainers, and undoes her school tie. She lays down on the grass and runs her hands and feet through it and looks up at the sky.*

JAY *enters.*

JAY. Pssst! Psst!

Come on!

DEE. Where have you been?

Lights out.

Seven

Day.

BEE, TEE *and* GEE *are outside the tent.* DEE *is visible sitting in it.*

TEE. She's not saying it's a problem.

DEE. Well, evidently she is.

TEE. No she's not.

GEE. She's just saying that we have all gone through something huge and we should talk about it.

DEE. There's nothing to talk about.

BEE. See!

TEE. You can't stay out here.

BEE. She doesn't care.

GEE. You're freaking your mum out, and you're freaking everybody out.

CHORUS. Stop!

What are you doing?

She's not ready yet.

You can't just stop the story.

I can.

You have to allow the story to unravel as it's supposed to.

Allow her to join the dots the way she needs to.

Yes but…

Yes but nothing! Let her go back! Let her trace her own steps. It's the only way she'll move forward.

She's drifting outside the realms of reality.

That's up for discussion.

But her memories are all over the place.

That's how memories work, there's no order to our memories.

Let's carry on.

Let her go through her own process.

Fine.

Fine.

Great.

Start them again.

It's dusk.

We know that!

Start them again.

Erm...

Where were we?

You're freaking everybody out?

Yeah!

GEE. You're freaking everybody out.

DEE. Well, everybody doesn't have to be around me, do they?

TEE. You have nothing to feel guilty about.

BEE. You really don't.

GEE. There's nothing you could have done.

TEE. Exactly.

GEE. Just come out.

TEE. Please?

DEE. No.

Eight

Night.

The CHORUS *enter from all over.*

CHORUS. My bra itches.

All of my bras itch.

Under my boob.

And my boobs are getting bigger.

I don't want them to be bigger.

Makes me look fatter.

DELETE.

It doesn't say delete.

It does.

It doesn't.

She erased it.

Happy?

Fine.

Recall it as it was written.

Fine.

Carry on.

My areolas are getting bigger too. My left areola's bigger than my right and I hate it.

It's not that I want my areola to look like everybody else's areola per se, it's just...

Well, I want it to...

Like...

Well, *not* look like the rubber on my HB. Know what I mean?

It's a *bit* scary, it's growing... I don't get it, don't want people to be scared.

Don't want fake-looking tits necessarily, don't wanna look plastic fantastic.

Don't wanna give people another reason to look at me in that way.

But I do want my tits to stand up.

Want them to be approachable. Know what I mean? I want *approachable* boobs.

Not like I would let just anybody approach them or anything... not like anybody will ever want to approach them, it's unlikely, I know that...

Just.

That.

I... I think I *ought* to have them ready for when someone is ready... like, if they ever are.

Sounds dramatic, but I don't care, that's what I want and I want to find someone that looks at me the way Granddad looks at Nan. And I want my mum to be happy again and I want to feel like I fit and feel the love people keep telling me they have for me, but I... don't.

I have dreams of flying, ya know.

Of closing my eyes, taking a big breath in, and soaring until I'm ready to come back down. Not as before.

Not gently.

A bang, come back down with a bang.

If I was braver I would... If I was braver I'd close my eyes and take a deep breath in and go.

I'd fly.

I'd soar until I was ready to come back down.

Not gently.

But with a bang.

If I was braver I'd make it all stop.

Nine

Dusk.

The Tent.

DEE *takes off her trainers, and undoes her school tie. She lays down on the grass and runs her hands and feet through it and looks up at the sky.*

JAY *enters.*

CHORUS. Sssh.

  DEE *lights a match and looks around once more.*

  She's doing it again, scrolling through pages, looking for answers, searching her mind for blossom seeds planted in memories.

DEE. Jay?

  JAY *lights a match in a completely different part of the space.*

  Lights out.

Ten

Dusk.

BEE. Get off the floor.

TEE. Get up off of the floor!

BEE. Quick!

TEE. Now!

DEE. Are you okay?

BEE. Of course she's okay.

DEE. No thanks to you.

BEE. And where were you?

DEE. Don't worry about where I was, worry why you were
    right by her side and you did nothing.

BEE. I wasn't by her side.

TEE. This isn't...

DEE. You were by her side.

JAY. Gee?

BEE. I wasn't by her side, if I was by her side I'd say I was by
    her side.

JAY. Gee, babe?

TEE. This isn't useful.

DEE. You were blatantly by her side doing absolutely...

BEE. I was not.

DEE. Absolutely nothing as per usual.

BEE. You're out of line.

DEE. I don't care, because you did absolutely nothing.

TEE. Can both of you shut up?!

DEE. She should leave.

TEE. Shut up!

JAY. We should…

TEE. Exactly.

JAY. We should take her to the hospital.

GEE. No!

JAY. She needs to go.

GEE. No.

BEE. We've got to tell her mum.

GEE. No.

BEE. We have to.

GEE. I said no.

BEE. Seriously.

DEE. She said no.

BEE. I heard her.

DEE. Then shut up.

BEE. What is your problem?

DEE. You, you're my problem, you're a liability.

BEE. Oh, I'm a liability?

JAY. Can you both just…

DEE. Yeah, *you*.

BEE. Coming from you, the one who…

TEE. Seriously…

BEE.…always gets us in some kind of mess…

TEE. If you're both gonna keep…

DEE. You wanna talk about mess?

BEE. Not really, that's your / job…

TEE. If you're gonna keep on arguing about absolute crap when she can barely…

DEE. You don't need to tell me.

TEE. She can barely open her…

DEE. I can see that.

BEE. You sure?

DEE. Why don't you shut your face?!

JAY. Both of you can shut up, seriously, you can both shut up and get lost!

> *Beat.*

Is that what you want?

BEE. I just want to make sure that she's alright.

JAY. Good.

GEE. Don't tell my mum.

JAY. Babe, we have to.

GEE. No.

TEE. She's right, we have to.

GEE. She'll only worry and I'm fine.

TEE. Seriously.

DEE. They're right.

BEE. Yeah, they are.

GEE. Please don't tell my mum. Seriously, for the last time, I'm fine, I will be fine.

JAY. Okay.

DEE. What?

JAY. We'll protect her.

DEE. Obviously! But that's / not the [point].

JAY. 'But' nothing. If she doesn't want to tell her mum, she doesn't have to.

BEE. Oh come on!

JAY. If we see anything again, we'll call the police. Until then, we protect her, we protect each other, like we always do.

TEE. This isn't the same.

DEE. Yeah… It really isn't.

TEE. Maybe, but we took an oath.

DEE. An oath?

JAY. Yeah!

BEE. A stupid promise when we were like five years old is hardly an oath.

JAY. Maybe not to you.

DEE. Babe, she's right.

JAY. Fine then, let's take one now.

DEE. This is ridiculous.

TEE. Don't know what has got in to you, but I'm telling her mum / and then I'm telling [the police].

GEE. Please, I'm begging you. It's not necessary. It was nothing serious… it just got a little out of control. Please…

TEE. No.

GEE. Please.

DEE. No.

JAY. That's final.

DEE. You don't get to decide.

BEE. This is ridiculous.

TEE. I don't want to be a part of this.

JAY. Then don't. If you can live with betraying one of your oldest friends then fine.

TEE. That's not fair.

JAY. She's asked us to do something, and we've gotta honour that, and it's as simple as that.

DEE. Fine.

JAY. Any final objections?

No reply.

Good!

Repeat after me.

I swear…

TEE. Nope.

GEE. I swear.

BEE. For God's sake, guys!

JAY. To stand with you.

GEE. To stand with you.

JAY. In all that you ask of me.

GEE. In all that you ask of me…

JAY. And to respect your wishes at all costs.

DEE. Fine.

ALL. And to respect your wishes at all costs.

JAY. Until the end of our friendships.

ALL. Until the end of our friendships.

JAY. Which will be never!

GEE. Ever!

JAY *places her pinky in the middle of the circle and waits.*

JAY. Well?

GEE *joins her pinky to* JAY*'s. Eventually all the* GIRLS *join in.*

Now, you're gonna text your mum and tell her that you're staying at Dee's.

DEE. What?

JAY. We all are!

DEE. My room's a mess.

JAY. Yes, but you're the only one without a nosey brother or sister and by the time it hits 9 p.m. your mum'll be on the wine / and forget about us!

DEE. Oi!

TEE. Sorted.

GEE. I love you.

BEE. I can't stand you.

JAY. She meant that!

BEE. Tart!

GEE. Cow!

Lights out.

Eleven

Day.

The cul-de-sac.

GEE, BEE *and* TEE *slump around the trolley.* DEE *paces. They are not as we have seen them before.*

The CHORUS *watch on, they are close.*

DEE. Right, you're me.

TEE. Fine.

DEE. And you're Jay.

GEE. Cool.

DEE. And we're gonna keep drilling this until…

BEE. Until what?

DEE. You don't need to be here if you don't want to.

BEE. Well, your mum told us to speak to you, she's worried.

DEE. Can we just get on with it?

GEE. Perhaps…

TEE. Perhaps we could talk.

GEE. Yeah.

BEE. Let us be there for you.

DEE. I remember how you liked to run.

GEE. I did?

DEE. Yes, she did. Now the crowd were roaring and she loved that. You loved that, right?

GEE. Yeah, yes, babe, I loved it.

DEE. And that was the last time, right?

TEE. Yeah.

DEE. And all of us came together, didn't we?

TEE. Yes.

DEE. I remember reading her message at like 8 a.m., what about you guys?

TEE. Well...

BEE. This is irrelevant.

DEE. I don't want you to talk to me any more.

TEE. It's fine, guys, I remember too, I think I read her message at like eight-thirty, does that sound right?

DEE. Yeah... I... I think.

TEE. Great.

DEE. Okay, so erm... I guess...

On your mark!

GEE. We're gonna start now?

DEE. Obviously!

GEE. Okay, babe.

DEE. On your mark!

Beat.

This isn't difficult, take your position... and the rest of you were not stood there, stand where you were.

GEE. Fine.

BEE. Look...

GEE *raises her hand and* BEE *acknowledges*.

DEE. Now you'd line us all up, make us sit and watch you race yourself so we were prepared, we knew where you would want us to be, and even though it was packed you could see us, you wanted us to watch you run, to feel free, and we did.

TEE. Pause.

DEE. No.

GEE. Just a quick pause.

DEE. All you guys have done since you arrived is pause, now you couldn't get it correct the first two times and so we're gonna get it correct now.

BEE. This is crazy.

DEE. So I'm gonna start again.

BEE. Whatever.

DEE. You'd line us all up, make us sit and watch you race yourself.

GEE. Sure.

DEE. Do you remember or not?

GEE. Yes, I remember.

Beat.

DEE. Continue.

TEE. We'd all have to sit there until you'd raced yourself at least ten times.

BEE. Yep.

DEE. And so… And so you start to run now.

GEE. Look… Pause.

DEE. No. Run.

GEE. Am I in the right place? Stand straight

Beat.

DEE. Answer her.

TEE. Yes.

GEE. Perfect.

TEE. On your mark!!! Get set!!! GO!!!   Start
                                          running

GEE *begins sprinting up and down the cul-de-sac.*

DEE. Faster!!!

TEE. So we... we chanted and you loved it and you were happy and...?

DEE. What do you mean, 'and'?

GEE. I keep going.

TEE. There's a point where you stop running because you're running out of breath.

BEE. And we cheer.

DEE. Good.

TEE. And we keep on cheering and cheering.

DEE. And you're feeling great, aren't you?

GEE. I think so.

DEE. You are.

GEE. Yes! I'm feeling great!

TEE. And you start to run out of breath again.

BEE. You do, you start to run out of breath.

TEE. You start to feel dizzy and you ask me to grab your water from your bag.

DEE. And she does.

TEE. Yep.

GEE. Do I stop now?

DEE. Are you running out of air?

GEE. I am.

DEE. Good, then you fall to the ground?

BEE. What?

DEE. She falls to the floor.

GEE. It's fine.   *I fall*

TEE. I give you water?

DEE. Yes.

TEE. And then what?

DEE. I... I'm not sure.

GEE. It's not okay. Let's go again.

TEE. No.

DEE. Just one more time.

TEE. No.

GEE. You couldn't have known, *we* couldn't have known.

DEE. That's crap, let's start again.

BEE. Maybe she just doesn't wanna be found, maybe that last day she felt freedom was when she ran, and she just didn't stop, maybe that was it.

DEE. Leave.

BEE. This didn't just happen to you.

DEE. I want you to leave.

BEE. Fine. But it won't bring her back.

TEE. It really won't.

Twelve

Dusk.

Enter DEE *and* JAY. JAY *pushes* DEE *around in a trolley. They are full of joy.*

The CHORUS *are close by.*

DEE. I want to go faster!!!

JAY. I'm trying!!

DEE. Try harder!!

JAY. I am!!!

DEE. Move your feet faster then!!

JAY. I am!

DEE. Even faster!

JAY. What if they fall off?!

DEE. They can't fall off.

JAY. But what if they do?

DEE. Then you have mankier feet than I thought!

JAY. My feet are beautiful!

DEE. They're dry like rhinoceros skin!

JAY. Shut ya face!

DEE. As dry as the Sahara!

JAY. You haven't even been to the Sahara!

DEE. Doesn't stop your feet being as dry as it!

JAY. Like your breath!

DEE. Like your foot!!

JAY. Like your lip in the winter!

DEE. LIKE YOUR RHINO FOOT! Spin me, Rhinoceros! Spin me round and round until my head rolls away from my neck!

JAY. You're so stupid!!!

> JAY *spins the trolley round.*

DEE. You're moving too slow!

JAY. Alright!

DEE. FASTER!!!

JAY. Shut up!

DEE. FASTER!

JAY. ALRIGHT!!!

> DEE *spins away from* JAY. *They both lose their balance and crash into a heap of laughter.* JAY *gets up to leave.*

DEE. Where are you going?

JAY. Look at the sky, babe!!! It's mental!!! Lay with me.

DEE. What?

JAY. Lay with me.

DEE. I don't remember this.

JAY. You do.

DEE. No, I would have remembered this.

JAY. But you do.

DEE. I don't.

> JAY *smiles.*

If I remembered, I'd say.

JAY. Okay.

DEE. No really I would.

JAY. It's okay.

DEE. 'Night, babe.'

   'Night, Rhinoceros.'

   'Look at the sky, babe, it's mental!'

JAY. Lay with me.

DEE. Don't wanna lay with you.

JAY. You do.

DEE. No.

JAY. You're scared, but you do.

   DEE *hesitates then lays down*.

DEE. What am I supposed to be looking at?

JAY. Just lay here.

DEE. I am.

JAY. Really be here with me, with the sky.

   DEE *grows annoyed and jolts up*.

   I told you.

DEE. No, you didn't.

JAY. I told you that I needed to go.

DEE. No, you didn't.

   I would remember.

JAY. I did.

DEE. No, I have gone over it and over it. I'd remember if you had, and I can't find that memory.

   JAY *smiles*.

JAY. Lay with me.

DEE. No.

JAY. Lay with me.

DEE. No.

JAY. Close your eyes and breathe.

DEE. No.

JAY *holds out her hand.*

JAY. Come on.

She waits.

DEE *gently lays beside her friend.*

Goodnight, babe.

DEE. Goodnight, Rhinoceros.

JAY. Look at the sky, babe, look how it paints the world. How it commands us to see it.

All seven-point-five billion of us.

Look at it, babe. Look how the clouds dance around the sun. How the moon pops up to say 'hi'. All of us reaching for the stars, reaching for the sky, trying to be red like the sky. Stand out like the sky.

To be heard like…

To roar like the sky.

To be seen, once again. Like the red in the sky.

Beat.

You see it, right?

DEE. No.

JAY. I asked you if you could see it and you said…?

DEE. What do you want me to say?

JAY. I asked you if you could see it and you said…?

DEE. No! I said 'no' because I couldn't!

JAY. Did you know there are like seven billion people on Earth?

Well, seven-point-five.

There are seven-point-five billion people on planet Earth.

As far as we know.

That's... nuts!

The CHORUS *appear in different spaces. In pairs. Looking to the sky. We bounce in and out of each of their worlds.*

CHORUS. I mean.

What does that even look like?

Like how can your brain even see that?

Like how can your brain even comprehend that?

Or even, hold that information...

What would we even do with that information?

If we could really understand it?

Contain it... hold it or... comprehend it...

Would we... try to connect more?

Become realigned...

Because, it's huge.

The idea that there are seven-point-five, or there are seven billion four hundred ninety-nine million nine hundred ninety-nine thousand nine hundred ninety-nine others... walking around, holding what I'm holding, trying not to fall down...

It's like...

You wanna say all these things like...

You plan to say all these things...

But your tongue gets caught on a...

What exactly?

Something... sharp!

Something like...

I guess...

What's the best way to say...

A hook!!

Yeah! It's like...

Suspended from the roof of ya mouth...

I'd imagine that would be uncomfortable...

And that's what I mean... I think.

No one wants a hook in their mouth...

Blocking their need to speak...

And then imagine if your fingers didn't work and you couldn't remove it.

And the muscles in your mouth had gone all floppy so you had to make sounds...

In an attempt to communicate...

To convey all of this ['everything-ness']...

Move your eyes up and down to convey all of this...

You'd do anything...

To be able to say...

To communicate...

To share... Or at least try to share the message...

...your message.

Sent from your brain to your mouth...

And if you couldn't communicate –

Or share the things that keep you awake at night.

The weight of your thoughts, your longing for elsewhere, what then?

JAY. You can't fix everything.

DEE. I can.

JAY. You can't and that's okay.

DEE. I can, though. If you had let me, if you would have allowed me to.

JAY. Let go, babe, go on.

DEE. No.

JAY. Yes.

DEE. No.

JAY. Yes!

DEE. Make me.

JAY. You sure?

DEE. Yeah, go on then!

DEE *pushes* JAY.

JAY *pushes her back.*

JAY. Don't make me take off my earrings and beat you up!

DEE. I'd like to see you try!

JAY. Let go, and stop being such a prat to the others, they love you.

DEE. Don't tell me what to do.

JAY. Stop acting like a spoilt brat then.

DEE. I'm not!

JAY. You are, babe.

DEE. I need you.

JAY. Let me go, Dee, let me go and remember how to play once again. Okay?

Beat.

Okay?

DEE. All that crap about sticking together.

JAY. It wasn't…

DEE. All that crap about looking up at the world together.

JAY. It wasn't crap.

DEE. You left me because you didn't believe in me.

JAY. That's not true.

DEE. You didn't give me a chance to help you. You didn't give me a chance to help you because you didn't believe in me.

JAY. You look proper strange when you cry.

DEE. WHAT?!

JAY. You can't fix everything, all of the time.

DEE. Stop talking in riddles, stop acting like I'm not supposed to miss you, stop acting like you haven't left me alone in this world, stop acting like we didn't fail you.

JAY. Lay with me.

DEE. No.

JAY. Just lean back, look up, watch how the clouds dance around the moon, how the heat from the day cools to make room for the night. Lay with me.

They fall back onto the grass.

DEE. Your breath smells like garlic.

JAY. Your breath smells like constipation.

They laugh.

At some point DEE curls into JAY and lays on her chest.

Slowly JAY gets up. She walks away.

The red from the sky lights us all.

Lights fade.

The End.